MW01153881

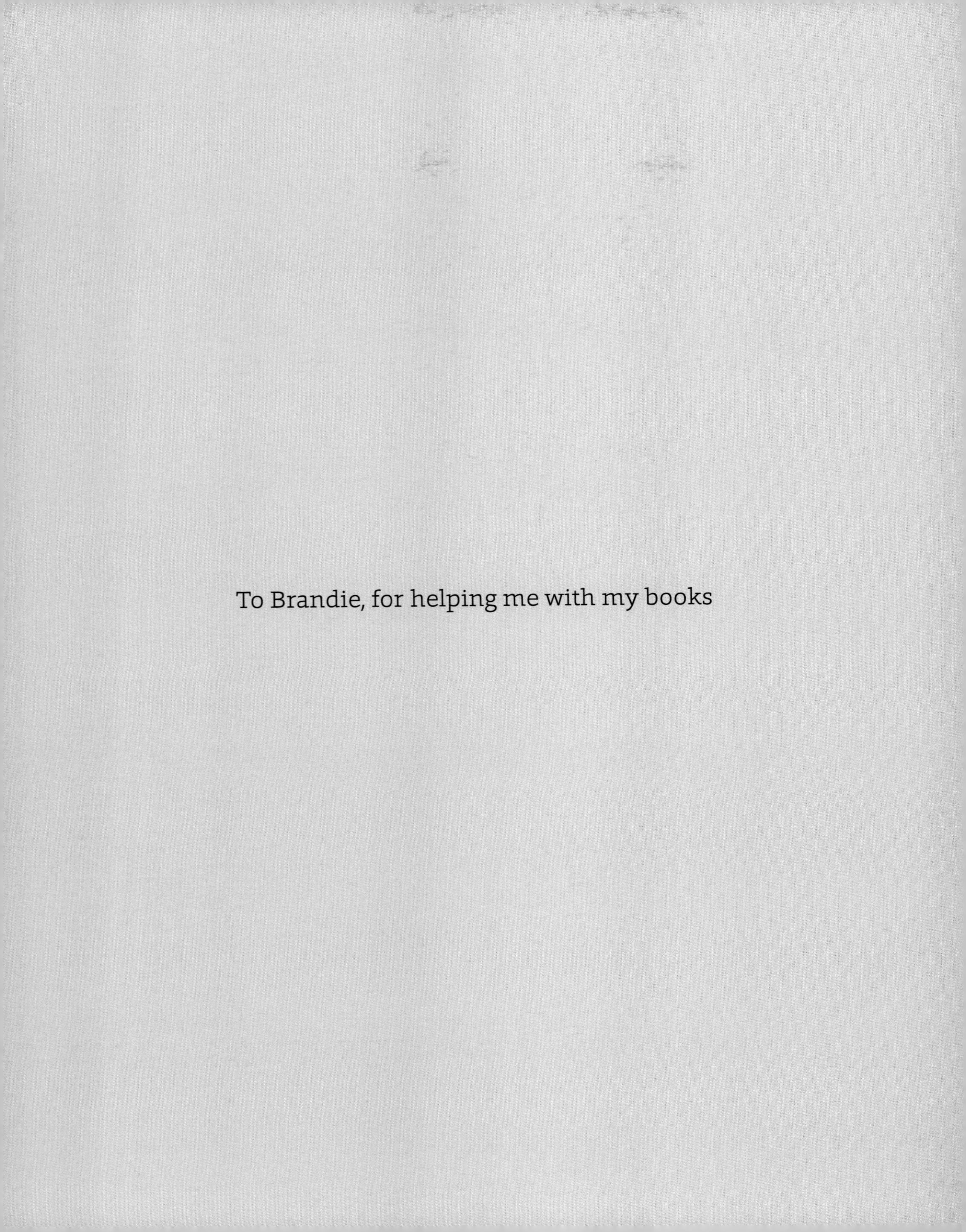
To Brandie, for helping me with my books

BAGGY EXPLORES WHITE SANDS

For more information, please contact:
Mascot Books
620 Herndon Parkway, Suite 320
Herndon, VA 20170
info@mascotbooks.com

Library of Congress Control Number: 2020900694

CPSIA Code: PRT0320A
ISBN-13: 978-1-64543-402-3

Printed in the United States

BAGGY
Explores White Sands

written and illustrated by P. S. Dickson

“Poppy, are you ready to go?” asked Baggy.

“Yep, you and Charlie can jump in the truck,” said Poppy.

While Poppy drove, Baggy helped.

"How long before we are in El Paso?" asked Baggy.

"Two days of driving," said Poppy.

Two days later, they picked up Mama and Maggie at the airport in El Paso.

Poppy, Mama, Maggie, Charlie, and Baggy were finally ready to go on their journey. They drove to White Sands Missile Range Headquarters and set up the camper.

White Sands Missile Range is still in use today. It is an open-air range where the United States Military and their allies research, develop, and test new defense technology.

The next morning, Baggy asked, “Poppy, can we go to the White Sands Missile Park and Museum now?”

“Yes,” said Poppy.

Mama said, “Remember, you can’t play on the missiles!”

At the park, the family saw a wide variety of missiles tested at White Sands Missile Range.

"Poppy, how old are these missiles?" asked Charlie.

“Some are from the 1970s,” said Poppy, “but some are from more recent testing. These Patriot missiles were used in the Gulf War in the 1990s.”

“Do they still test missiles and rockets today?” asked Maggie.

“Yes, sometimes the road between here and Alamogordo is closed while they hold testing,” said Poppy.

The family walked along the park's nice path. No one was allowed to climb on the missiles, rockets, and planes.

"Baggy! Get down!" yelled Mama.

After everyone finished looking at the rockets and missiles, the family went back to their campsite. Baggy, Maggie, and Charlie played at the playground. Then they had a campfire.

The next day it was time to move to a new campsite.

"Where are we going today, Mama?" asked Baggy.

"We're going to Oliver Lee Memorial State Park," said Mama.

The drive was only about an hour north from White Sands Missile Range.

Oliver Lee Memorial State Park is located at the base of the Sacramento Mountains. The park offers a wide variety of activities including hiking and visiting a historical ranch house.

“Poppy, did real Apache Indians live here?” asked Baggy.

“Yes, back in the 18th century,” said Poppy.

“Mama, can we go to White Sands National Monument today?” asked Charlie.

“Yes, that is the plan for today,” said Mama.

White Sands National Monument is located on US-70 between Alamogordo and Las Cruces, New Mexico. The White Sands monument is in the Tularosa Basin and is one of the world's great natural wonders.

“Are we at the beach?” asked Baggy.

“No,” said Poppy.

“Why is it so white like the beach?” asked Charlie.

"The wind and sun have broken down the gypsum to make the white sand," said Poppy.

“What is gypsum?” asked Baggy.

“A long time ago, this area was covered in water. When the water was gone, gypsum was left,” said Poppy. “Over many years it has broken down to white sand.”

Baggy, Charlie, and Maggie had fun sledding on the white sand.

“WATCH ME MAMA!” yelled Baggy.

After several more days, Mama and Poppy packed up the camper.

"Where are we going now Mama?" asked Baggy.

"It's time to go home, baby!" said Mama.

TEXAS
Let's GO

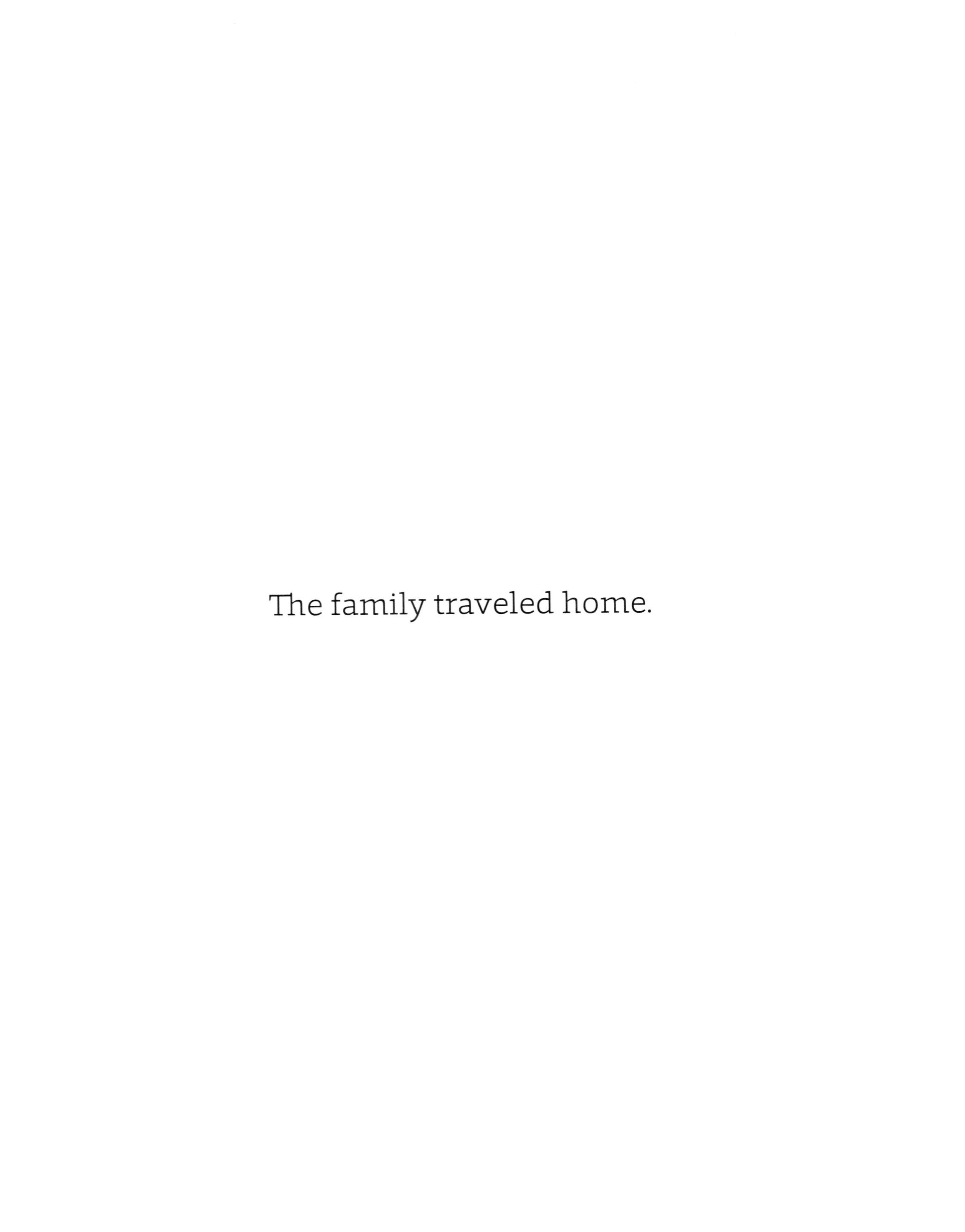

The family traveled home.

Plan a Trip to White Sands

WHITE SANDS NATIONAL MONUMENT

www.nps.gov/whsa/planyourvisit/directions.htm

OLIVER LEE MEMORIAL PARK

www.emnrd.state.nm.us/SPD/oliverleestatepark.html

WHITE SANDS MISSILE RANGE US ARMY POST

www.wsmr.army.mil/Pages/home.aspx

WHITE SANDS MISSILE RANGE MUSEUM

www.wsmr-history.org

KOA

koa.com/campgrounds/alamogordo

BOOT HILL

www.boothillrv.com

CAMPING NEAR WHITE SANDS MISSILE RANGE

(Active and retired military can camp at the US Army Post)

www.blm.gov/visit/aguirre-spring-campground

About the Author

After teaching first grade and kindergarten for 29 years, I wanted to create content that would impact children and families forever. My husband Dennis and I enjoy traveling across the United States in our RV and checking off national parks and monuments, and I wanted to encourage more families to travel and get outdoors. Our goal is to one day visit all of the national parks.

We enjoyed many years of traveling and camping with our daughters, Brandie and Brittney, who are now grown and raising families of their own. Now, we travel with our fur children: Baggy, a black cat; Charlie, a black lab; and Maggie, a Pomeranian.

I hope you will join us on all of our adventures!